QUINQUENNIUM

A Collection of Poems by George Horsman

CONTENTS

Conception 1

Gravity 2

Illusion 3

Canals of Old London 4

Sight Unseen 6

Fishing.. 7

A Pleasant Seat.. 8

Summit 9

Tristan da Cunha 10

Rising Star Caves, South Africa 11

Out, Not Out... 13

Out of the Mouth.. 14

Suggestibility 16

Last Payment... 17

Time 18

Very Well, Then. Alone... 19

A Slip in Time... 20

A Lament for Lowry 21

All Found 22

Repayment 23

Grief.. 24

My Photographer, My Love... 25

Hands Off... 27

Extraordinary 28

Shaving 29

If Only 30

Company 31

From Scratch... 32

Dogs.. 33

Breathing... 34

The Tempest 36

Names 37

Union Pacific 38

Goodbye, Daughter.. 39

St Kilda 40

Toys 41

Which Way? 42

Disadvantaged... 43

The Bad News.. 44

Love 45

Edgware Road, 7 July 2005 46

Dagmar 47

Doughboys, 8 May 1945,............................... 48

Granddaughters.. 49

Ammonite Fossil.. 50

Throwback 51

Not Out 52

Snow 53

Brief Encounter.. 54

'Someone to see you.' 55

Make-Believe 57

Balloons 58

Pied Piper of Hamley's 59

Glasgow Necropolis: Best of Both Worlds.............. 61

Take-aways 62

Design Fault 63

To My Daughter.. 64

Review 65

Costs and Benefits.. 66

Love, Hope, Recompense 67

Inventory for Andromeda.. 69

Desiderata.. 71

The Night DJ 72

And Yet So Far 73

Rain 74

Sugar Boat... 75

Mary 76

Reversal... 77

For the Little-Read 78

Retirement, Release 79

Upper Room 80

A Hanging... 81

Thoroughness 82

Mid-Life Stasis.. 83

Giving Back 84

Nos Et Mutamur in Illis 85

Turtle Station. 87

Tenement 89

Alpine Man, ... 90

Eternal Triangle 92

Identity 94

Lies 96

Words That Say Nothing 97

Valentine... 98

Truth 99

Ten Days Before 100

Blessed Siren 101

Loyalty 102

Rainfall 103

John Donne 104

Dear Descendant, ... 105

Pompeii 106

The Hint 108

Fort McMurray, 2016 109

Piecing England Together............................ 110

My Novel 111

Minister.. 113

On Becoming a Grandad 114

Given, Taken Away 115

Plus Ca Change 116

Cortege 117

Nocturne 118

Paradise 119

Kin.. 120

Christmas Eve 121

Darkness Visible 122

Curriculum Vitae... 123

Conception

Liking waking a hedgehog buried in deep grass
or shy in a wreath of roots. Rather like that.
Or like the idea for a poem that slowly uncurls
in the mind at early dawn, not quite awake
but in that magic-carpet world
where past and present interfuse and make
all futures – all those multifarious many –
already here, this hour. Why does he now
nestle inside me, unproved yet past all doubt,
for whom we tried so often, never yielding
success, until we signed, went to the shop
and bought a boy? And from then on,
as if creation sipped from his small cup,
the spark was lit. Tonight we have built a tower,
this little fellow and I, slid the last carriageway
across the central gap in a bridge
a thousand feet high. I lie, feeling the mite unfledged
in my deep core, a stranger yet at home,
and I can't tell from whom he has most come –
from me, my lover, or you, my adopted boy,
father of my son.

Gravity
(For those who walk in space.)

Never was night so black,
never stars such tiny
pinholes of salt-dust spray.
Below –
but here is no below, no above;
up and down link with nothing
in the lost grope of space –
the earth's wisps, white, green, blue,
dazzle as its huge crescent belly curves
with infinite gradation into the void.
Never was silence so still.
If the voice of God were ever to be heard
it would be in this place.
And yet there is no place, no co-ordinates
to grapple to, only this motorless turning.
At the snap of nylon, a terror,
a grabbing for hold, and then
as hope froze to an end
the resignation of peace.
So this is to die,
this is the way it comes. I could reach out
and grasp you, pendulous earth, small universe.
I could peel off the thin blue rind of your atmosphere.
I could write poetry in these closing hours.

Illusion

Derwent Water at the approach of night
pulls magic tricks from her sleeve.
A pinpoint of light on the far shore
stakes a barred column, as bright
as some flaming pillar of fire,
in the water beneath.

A huge, mauve horizontal slice
of hilltop becomes detached and turns
upside down in the lake, the lower slopes
unmirrored, cut off by some nice
mystical quirk of sunset. A burn
thrusts out from the hillock behind a copse

and builds across the surface a long
black jetty of flow, a mirage on which
real boats are moored, pictures pinned
as cartoon cut-outs superimposed upon
the face of fantasy, wizard on witch,
sign of our never knowing water from wind,
matter from mind.

Canals of Old London

They are my veins, these canals of old London,
and our boat a cholesterol blob
that flakes from the water-wall and bobs
under bridges and through wide parks
dumbed from the hiss and drum
of the capital's ceaseless quake.

Here, edging aside, we pass by Jason,
his *Argonaut* forever at war
with scrap kids who pelt him with stones
and call him names and tell his passengers
his is 'a golden fleece'. In Paddington Basin
at Little Venice the nannies sit alone

except for pram or pushchair or a toddler
leashed on a leather strap.
Au pairs from Umbria or the Ardeche
(here to find boyfriends, penniless as crap)
draw slanted shade from the mansions of old codgers
who spare no glance as they leave for the Square Mile's
                                                    rush.

Huddled behind King's Cross, we could get out
and, entering a pub through grass at its back door,
be ethered into a world
so rural as to draw
no notice from the maggot-seething crowd.
But now darkness unfurls

overhead as we tunnel below the criss-cross
of rails and platforms the Victorians left.
This day could be our last. Should we meet
one booming barge our voices would be lost
under the engine-roar. We would be swept
into the chill and soak. Our street's

one way, there's no returning. But there arrives
nothing to ram us. And in these slack
backwaters of an ever-rampant age
we become Orpheus, lured here by a rage -
to escape change, commotion, the fake wise -
moored to the dark, forbidden to look back.

Sight Unseen

Blind, he is not alone. He lives here with the sounds.
Sark has no cars, but every wave
washing the rocks, raking the ground
like fingers through tousled hair, is individual
as a face in a crowded hall,
breath in a hushed cave.

Across the island someone hammers home
a nail, mis-hits, hammers it straight again
and over a mile of hillside everything
is heard and understood. A child is playing
a violin. With *Twinkle, star* comes
every note of his tiny fingering.

Smells, too: fresh foliage of spring,
scent of night-fallen rain, horse manure
on the shining road. The distant lowing
of a cruise ship across the twenty miles of sea
that cut off France. In winter you're
alone with warmth and peace while storm and sky

whip fury round the panes and you
snuggle ecstatic here. And the mainland past
cradling your infant life before you quit
still glows: red pillar box, green gorse, the blue
of icicles spiked on the sky, all lost
for night's dark friendship and the loves it lit.

Fishing

'No, I don't really fish. It's just,
it gets me out of the flat.
I'm ninety, you know.'
I didn't, but might have guessed,
as I guessed that our minute's chat
on the canal-bank where we met,
a rod in his hand, a wide-brimmed hat
shading a sago face, in his mind would grow
bigger than any other event that day,
perhaps his sole words spoken. Anxiety
about the government, income tax, new laws,
would scarcely pass his door,
only the aching emptiness
of a life with no one to embrace,
only the echo of thoughts
wrung from the past. He told me all of that –
the war in which he'd fought,
his eight-year illness, a fiancee's death.
I paused and let
him ramble, for our meeting was
his imprint in the sand, a breath
into the carrying wind, a stand
against the dwindling murmur of things gone,
his ninety-year defiance against death.

A Pleasant Seat
(for Chester)

First, a small necklace of red stone
with no suburb attachments beyond,
puissant, aglitter with the hope of the young,
against surround of dark forest and moorland
where any wolf or bear might have its home.

Then complacent county seat
of the northern Marches, a local lordling
with Chancellor, Abbot, Earl,
huntsman in her own lands, their purlieus affording
wide prospects of power and height.

Third came the overtake
by billow of sulphurous smog
among rivalrous neighbours, the clank
of rail, hammer, drill, chainsaw, cog,
engines' steam and shriek.

Last, aged now, a second childhood
with second strength flowing back, a return of blood,
a coming into her own, a wife
who discovers herself when her tyrant husband dies
and builds in her heart a refuge, a dignity
in these walls which encircled my life.

Summit

Ah, komm ein, Robin. We expect you.
Your usual seat, yes? Your journey was good?
Yes, fifty years now since The Day,
you in the third wave after the taken bridge.
You don't forget, no – nor we either –
the thing that's biggest in your life. And sure,
this battle tilts the war and you
played part in it. Some wine, yes?
So we drink up. No, Elke, she is ill,
not so young now. We all aren't.
How long you keep it up, this every-year
visit to us in Clodheim? For ever, you think?
Good. So it should be. And tonight you stay
before you go back to your house in England?
So, it is settled. Before bed, we drink.

I think he is failing, Elke. Such small man
to bear such weight. But most I fear he lose
the joy of being Someone on that day
those years since, when his tank rumbles into
our town. Since then, nothing has mattered.
It is his highest place, his Matterhorn.
And it will break him if one smile of pity
he sees on our faces, or if we shall come
to life's end first and leave him
with no one knows his fame;
or if, in giddying age,
we live forgetting.

Tristan da Cunha

*(Farmers returning to the island after a volcanic
eruption advertised for land-girls.)*

I felt I'd brought her luck
(though luck she'd have to earn)
at first, walking arm in arm
down the aisle, she making me
her husband after the shock
of the island's eruption calmed
and we sealed my return.
Coming back to the farms
we needed women – and how! –
on this out-jutting rock
in the relentless sea
with never a skirt or breast
in sight. Even just company…
Our ads did all the rest.

But now the pride has slipped.
Land-girls, we said, but in
less than three months they all
were married women.
A summer sale, you might call
it, a market if ever was one.
And what I feel is, I trapped
mine, as the others did:
healthy for making kids,
vigorous in kitchen and bedroom,
but brought here like produce
to cook, clean, help, give birth
yet live like some recluse
in a far, mountain cave,
bound by her vows to stay
where she can't want to live
yearning her years away
on this infertile earth.

Rising Star Caves, South Africa

'Things wonderful,'
Howard Carter breathed,
opening the Pharaoh's tomb.
As we do now. Visceral-deep beneath
Africa's grassy uplands, a vision so like
Carter's in starting quake
of heart and lung, but its earth
as different as the moon.
We broach the cave's hunched arch,
its blackness pierced by the prong
of head-bound torch;
we crawl through half-clamped jaws
of granite, totter over
plunges to darkest space,
then trust to grip and rope
in the gaping gullet's void.
And here we plumb sights untold,
unseen in two million years
since these lonely, laid-out bones
were left to their gods, their Fate.
Discarded, undraped they lie,
yet placed with a deference
speaking a formal death,
a ceremony in dust.
This man took nothing for his journey,
no weapon, no household thing,
no finery, no ring,
and yet his household must
have issued commands somehow.
Even lacking words, surely they knew
to pass on fear or hope,
to yelp the protective shout
in warning of attack
or pass farm or foodstuff facts
from one prognathous snout
to another.

This was a woman.
So small. So childlike. We grope
in the cave-floor's crumble, the bare
shatter of rock that rattled
her backward-sloping skull
in its gunfire hail.
And we ask: are you one of us,
small lady? What did they think
who bore you here in loss,

leaving no gold, no charms,
not dreaming the years would link,
after so many dawns,
you with us *sapiens*,
who now with reverence
and the silent throat of awe
gently process you hence?

Out, Not Out

The phone rings and somewhere
a man out in Bangkok,
Capetown or Bangalore
or - just as gobbledygook -
Gateshead or Edinburgh
garbles out some mangled greeting.
'George Horsman speaking,'
I say, and they,
with the robot ineptitude
that clogs their kind, reply,
'May I speak Mr Horsman?'
For fullness they append,
'I am not selling anything.'
But they always are, or want
my bank account number or PIN, and after
a tangle with the voice from Spain
or Punjab or Bloemfontein,
at last in cold calm I release
the words I've long longed to use
to shut out all life's woes.
As a batsman at the crease
stonewalls the hours away
under hurtled deliveries,
'Sorry, not here,' I say.
'Mr Horsman's not here today.'

Out of the Mouth
(for my grandson, Dylan)

Minute bundle, scarcely findable in your cot,
boxing-glove small but growing
with each voracious suck, you open out
the future like a party popper, blowing
imagination till it stretches far beyond
the years I'll live to see, past the century's end.

And yet you're a history-maker.
With your tiny pimple of nose and puckered lips
you're a Chinese sage – slant-eyed, once in a while
nodding in shrewd appraisal of some data
your brain has processed, or, tipsy
with thoughts your eyes can't bring to focus, cracking a
                                                    smile.

You'll never know how precious to me that smile is.
All else – the tuft of grandpa hair,
the chubby, pianist's hands, the feet
already kicking for Arsenal – are deliveries
of genes from others in your pedigree;
but a smile's a sun that rises everywhere

and shines on everyone. Little man,
I hold your head clear of clonking; kiss a sea-shell ear
so delicate it could hear
the far tide turning. I worship your yawn,
absurd with its toothless ramp
of gums, crimson as dawn.

And I wish you luck. You're going to need it.
In the world you, young Confucius, have entered
almost anything can happen, and in fact
normally does. But keep on smiling. Remember:

when you've spent your purse of brains, strength, charm
                                                and tact,
luck's just a name for effort long-repeated.

Suggestibility

The day I saw you in your skin-tight pants
on the 19 bus to Battersea
was, by chance, the day the flying ants
pupated and came out, invading the pantry

and living room like a parachute regiment,
but soon scattered, and me their slaughterer.
Now, with the glisten-winged and crawling wounded sent
to a crushed death, there still appears

a rare lonely survivor. And just as that sight
alone brings imagining's itch over me,
so a taut bicep or a purse stretched tight
triggers my body with your memory.

Last Payment
(for Tony Palmer (1931-2016))

'Tell him I kept my promise.'
I gave it when he asked it
at our last meeting, the week after he learnt
his growth drew a curtain closed. Yet it wasn't that
that nudged me on to make the trip
to see him, only that, old friends, we weren't

able to meet much and it seemed,
well, about time. He knew –
always had known – his dreams
of God and heaven and all the rest
found in his holy book were alien to
my way of thought: and yet

he asked, 'Please, pray for me.'
And for this once I didn't express
puzzlement or the old ironical surprise
at his deep earnestness
to avoid a realm he saw as paradise,
and so I answered, 'Yes, I will.' And did,

though whether prayer made by the unbelieving,
even with the bitter lemon of doubt
anaesthetised, would pack much punch
curdles a doubt. But I kept my word, relieving
his need for love. For from a friend that much
is the least payment due when we go out.

Time

As a razorbill slashes a lancet-line
with fine precision across the face of the mere
to speed-trap squirming prey,
or as funicular, pregnant raindrops wobble their way
down the descending slope of guyrope or wire,
the present moves in time,

a Euclidean point, a speck
stripped of all magnitude, lasting no tick
of clock or watch.
Yet our entire life's lived there. It's all
we have, this nothingness, edged from the stage
like a bad actor, dropped beyond recall

before he's time to speak. And yet
so priceless, so unique a time we reject
and choose to stand
clogged by tomorrow's fears or past's rebound
while *now*'s wealth-laden clipper dims beyond
the sight of land.

Very Well, Then. Alone

Inside, I totter. Can I run
this smuggler trade alone,
bear alone the smithereen nights,
stalk-eyed with sleep's extinction?
In the waking dark come moments when
I shake, amazed the law allows
me to do this, a thief
of new life brought larcenous
to a woman unknown to men.
There's anger and defiance. Yet with it delight,
an unsteady and too-bright fulfilment,
a giddy trembliness.
Where does he live, the lover I never met
who creamed the lab-glass?
Will the speck in me one day want
to know where he began –
or, failing, corrode with loss?
I fight back. He or she won't
ever, at least, lack love, unlimited as the sky.
And he'll be mine, all mine,
wherever the alien genes
erupted from. Yet there is pity, too,
pity for the fatherless. The path
to all-negation posed no cliff-side way.
Yet, men having slipped my gaze,
in snubbing birth I would have faced
deserts without oasis, forty more
solitaire years, a journey without trace.
Lack of one love shouldn't entrain another.
Often in the night, measuring the cost
of innocence, I summon
as guides my father, my brothers,
sole immigrants from that unknown
land of men, that remote island
where I shall never reach coast.
Is not to know it utterly trivial,
a shrugged omission? Or a whole world lost?

A Slip in Time

*(The Large Hadron Collider in a circular tunnel near
Geneva, re-creates the state of the universe one billionth
of a second after its creation).*

One billionth. Compared with which
the batting of a silverfish's eye
unrolls eternity. Under this soil,
part French, part Swiss,
the particles clash,
armies at war, their swords
incandescent, infinitesimal,
an arc-weld universe
in battle.

      One billionth.
We might trust
the French to be so late. But then
suppose through some mistake,
some fine miscalculation,
the hair-line crack was bridged
and time pushed back
one billionth, to that edge,
that causeless cataract,
that bulging birth.
In that hour wouldn't we
by our own hand create
a new heaven, a new earth?

A Lament for Lowry
(for L.S.Lowry, 1887-1976)

They gather round me wherever I stop and paint,
small kids from the gutters who haven't had a wash
for weeks. They ask me who I am or ain't
and what I'm doing, sketchbook or brush
in hand. Why do I draw
the drab, chewing-gum-stretched-out streets
with opening-on-the-pavement doors?
They seem to meet
my need for company. Mainly, I sketch
People Standing Around or *Leaving t'Mill*
or, one of my best, *Goin' to t'Match.*
They are my friends, that lonely spill
of scarves and cloth caps, and the cripples
left over from the war, an arm missing here,
one legless on a wheeled board, one who grapples
a tearaway dog. Through them appears
my hollow life. And when rain starts
its somehow comforting fall and I move off, the kids
follow. They are my family. From them nothing's hid,
no loss, no loneliness, no grief of the heart.

All Found

So comfy in here – the perfect hideaway.
Around me the soft pad and paddle of waters,
the bend and bulge of this sac
pliable as a lawyer's argument,
the soothe of warm water-bottle.
Fed and quenched through this serpentine tube,
I don't open my eyelids or blink
but light still filters in, as to fishes
– indigo, blue, yellow, crimson –
who laze in tropical shallows,
or rise from deep ocean fissures
to be blessed by the sun's warmth.
I hear sounds, too. Once I and this other
(I'm not alone in here; there's some huge being
around me – the voices call it 'mother')
heard the rising swell of music
and at one word – *Hallelujah*, was it? –
I kicked my legs in thrill and felt
a sudden shifting of weight
as if by my kick some load had been displaced
from the shelf it rested on.
But fear comes through, as well. Often I've clenched
my fists to walnuts and pummelled
these rubbery walls,
shouting against feared change. Yet week by week
my head turns down, drawn by a need to dive,
without sound or breath, out of this cave's embrace
and deep-drenched comfort.
I live here free, all found,
yet alarmed by threat of chute
into some world of fear, alarm, affront,
a world I've never known.
I purse my lips. I scowl.
No, I will not be moved.

Repayment

Once, she let go of me
as I went off on my bike, wobbly
and perilous. There had to be that minute.
There was the day when, at the school's entry,
she hung back so that I, at ten, wouldn't be
ashamed of needing her. And yet I did.

There was a night when she
came, as she always did, to my bedside
'to say goodnight', but really
to help the poisons of the street
and school die down, to soothe the pain inside.
Yet that night we barely met,

split by my stoniness, my imperious wish
to be grown-up. After that she didn't
come again. The folly of it
aghasts me still: to trash
so buttressing a tie, as precious
as any life brought, rubbished in the ditch.

And now I let go of her. No choice
is offered me, just as it never
was offered her. There has to be goodbye.
Her pulse fades, then her voice.
Now, in this moment, she steps free
and all the world sings to tumultuous heaven.

Grief

When you rang and told me your man was dead
I heard my voice deepen with the laboured tread
of a steam train setting off,
the billows stabbing and choking puff by puff.
And a cold wind of guilt
cut through the lightweight jacket I had on,
so that I tried to think only of John's merits,
not his shortcomings – not to see him sport
the consciousness of virtue like a coat
made heavy by freeze of rain,
stiffened to vitreous. But what had fitted
well enough during forty years now seemed little
more than his aid to blindness towards all
you meant and were. I tried not to recall
our stolen weekends, mine and yours,
in the rise and sweep of the Dales
by Swale, Ure, Wharfe and Ouse,
the castles we climbed to, their secret keeps and baileys,
the hidden, tower-high rooms. So in fractured voice
I spoke my sorrow, my proxy for penitence,
while among limestone fells and the crags' grey height
a wolf of joy howled under dawning light.

My Photographer, My Love

(for R.O. from one who knew him well)

It's through your photos that I love you.

Like that chill day in Prague when we first met,
I scribbling the tumult, you pressing the camera catch,
as the crowds in a kind of angry independence,
a hopelessness against hope,
shifted and swirled below Wenceslas's armour,
proud on his horse and plinth, undeniable,
a statement of all they longed for,
a reservoir dam at its burst;
and you bought grade-three wine and we drank
in that same half-hope, as unsure of ourselves
as the crowd of their destiny.

Like the time the sinister tower, a 'gift' from Stalin
gaunt in surveillance over Warsaw, was suddenly decked
with advertising and became
merely more tat of the capitalist West
on your tabloid rag's front page.

Like our day with the baby rhino
at Leipzig Zoo, he sitting astride
the boulder head of his mother
mildly interested in her tusk-horn
- a future that beckoned him.
And having no duties further,
we drank coffee in the aquarium
and watched spheres of myriad silk fins
travail and turmoil and ballroom
in the Zoo's and our own underwater.

Like our night under the stars, a celestial duvet,
watching and making fast the Transit of Venus,
a necklace of bright planets across the face of the sky;
and you picked in Hyde Park a daisy chain

and hung it about my waist
thinking of Lady Chatterley.

Like our watch on that vagabond comet
that headed for us like a bull or fierce lover
but, robbed of its conquest, was lured
into the far-flailing gases of Jupiter,
plopping into his breast with a splash
two thousand miles high. That conquest, too.

So many. On the big wheel, you St Catherine
close to broken with fright. You in the car perspiring
with unease at meeting my mother. You
calling me all your names: *my penguin,
my pouter, my mouse.*

For all these photographs in my mind and in your acetate
I love you, indelible, immortal,
my Mercury, my messenger of the gods.

Hands Off

I know. It's fun, isn't it,
twisting my nose, my muzzle,
as if to find out if it turns me on?
Well, no. It doesn't.

They don't turn off at night,
either, those hands of yours, but stay
even in your deepest sleep
stretched up, pointing at stardust
sprinkled in the Milky Way.
They're probes you've not yet mastered
but leave switched on, alight,
at close of day.

And when your baby-carriage goes
under a garden beech
you bubble, a boiling stream,
and grasp the rustling air under its boughs,
pulling them down to your reach.

They'll be your precious tools
for life, those sandworm fingers there,
with hammer, paintbrush, ivories, pen,
a loved one's cheek and hair.

But now they twist my nose
to see the effect, your first experiment.
No, NOT my eyes, wee shrimp,
not those!
I may need them.

Extraordinary

People don't see a miracle,
don't calculate
or comprehend it.
Today, for instance, I saw
(think of the odds against it!)
the one, sole number-plate
marked *YV 314*!

Shaving

Not as one pans a sausage in the kitchen
or frees a carrot from its bed, but in
that clash of care with flushing awkwardness
one might feel picking up a toad, the nurse
bends to her task. For a moment the toad
- or slug, more like – stirs, and in crisis mode
she flicks a nail to quell it, a tactic learnt,
one feels, but not deployed before. The burn
of soap in steaming water and the grazed
soreness of pink gooseflesh. The op-site rased.
A dab of cotton towel, then she's thrown
her rapier in the basin and she's done.

How quickly shame died! What had seemed
lifetime humiliation now recedes
- like its chief object – from supreme disgrace
to a brief haircut for a commonplace
and functional appendage in a nest
that only constant cover rendered modest.
All this with gaze averted. Only when
she's leaving do our eyes join hands and then
a stickleback smile twinkles to me from her.
A joke? A secret shared? An *au revoir*?

If Only

Now it's too late to say, I think
it all the oftener. If only
I'd taken a deeper breath, seized
courage all those times when my heart sank
for fear of looking a fool; if I'd stepped
up to the crease. It was the hanging behind
that really made me feel a fool, and lonely.
That and fear of defeat.
But rivalry's not a good friend
for love; the two don't meld.
You'd need a metamorphic change of mind
for knuckle-fights to jostle with the swoon
of angel-worship. I'm not that kind.
And so, why bother? The missed bus has gone.
Better seek future fortitude
than shed tears for the waning of the moon,
now it's too late to say *I love you.*

Company

Zigzagged in the head, before making an end,
he flung wide the cages of his private zoo
and, sniffing new air,
the lions, tigers, bears panhandled out.
Why the stubbing-out of his days? We've no reply.
But before he probed the gun
against his temple, from their prison slunk
that terror of creatures, untrustful, one by one.
Guilt for their lifelong prison
perhaps was too hard to bear, or maybe
mere pity racked him that they should
be given some chance to roam,
following their nature, to hunt for food,
enjoy a fleeting freedom
for evil or good.

Lacking the means of capture, the cops could only kill.
A charnel field, they left.

And I ponder:
had he foreseen their end, his fellow-prisoners,
would he have gone to death so soon?
Or in conscience revolted back?
Or at the least passed on
in greater peace for knowing
he did not go alone?

From Scratch

Congratulations, wee man.
You've reached twelve weeks and already
you can focus your eyes
and hold your head almost steady.
And the sheer ecstasy
of your songs without words, now you can

convey what you mean by a burble
or by kicking your legs or a gurgle
of your toothless smile! We grumble
together and you gaze at my snout
in disbelieving amusement. You're in doubt,
even despair, wondering

who this old chap can be. You stretch out your hand
and touch the sight, prod the sound, hear
the aroma of Cussons or Pears.
All in twelve weeks. And still there's
so much to learn. Even your Grandad
- and he's past his seventieth year –

learns a thing or two every day.
So much – not to become
a nuclear whizzkid-sage or play
Steinway in the Festival Hall
but only to manage a home,
a job, a wife, that's all.

So keep on learning, my grandson.
And tell Mum – you know, that funny old one –
to keep on inviting me over
to see you and swap what we've done.
If she kicks up a fuss we'll have fun
running for cover.

Dogs

on the beach at the low point of the tide
scatter wide circles, skitter and skid
and join in mock-joust and battle.
There's no draining their energy and muscle
as, for eyes that move
barely a foot above
the level of shining sand, the skyline spreads forever
to America, Newfoundland
and north under scimitar horizon
to the ice-corseted Pole.
Green frills of sea scrabble their paws.
But what strikes most is their *presentness*.
They never pause
in their zigzag game
with its sudden plant of feet and rear of mane,
or care that the dug-in stamp
into all-imprinting sand
crumbles at the next wave.
From their efforts nothing's saved;
only corrugate ridges remain.
They move like Jurassic beasts,
unforeseeing, unrecorded,
freed from time, finding peace
in non-prescience, rewarded
by an everlasting *now*.

Breathing

I tiptoe in. The bars of your cot
cast bulrushes of dark across your coverlet
from the gentle dance of the night-light. But

what I want to be near
isn't the joy of the eye, only the ear –
the sound of your breathing. I hear

it even before I've nudged the door closed:
soft yet unrestrained, one of those
faint, distant cries a train howls across

canyons of the Rockies or through the forest
that spreads its endlessness
over Canadian wastes dark to the west.

But it's the movement of time, not space,
that makes the infant tinkliness
of your cough arrest,

like the memory of a voice
unheard since being a boy,
brimful of schooldays' echoes;

or of times after that: the breath
of children achase in the heather
during hot summer days on the heath;

the night's low music from breast
of lover or wife; or the last
as-if-drowned sinking to rest

at close of her threescore years
– plus or minus a few, a mite more or less –
when time laid its last caress

on a mother's stutter of heart,
on the rattle-cough and the hard
path to the all-forget.

The Tempest

Hard as it is for someone in our time
to hear a fairy tale with spells,
spirits and magic; hard, too, to bear
long staircarpets of speech; still the deeps move
as the last curtain strews some breath-held
inklings of freedom - Ariel's from servitude,
Prospero's from the island, some from crime,
and we from lives that never take to the air,

forever enmired. In this the poetry helps –
reminds us of the fog-enclosed cocoon
we live our days in; reminder, as well,
how all we know's intangible as light,
the solid world built from our fivefold senses
like a child's card-house. What lives on
is this drenched island's charm, which gives delight,
sounds and sweet airs, and brings nobody ill.

Names

After six years apart she shed my rings
diamond and golden, filtered down her letters
to a sparse holly-card at Christmas, halted
pleas that I should devote more time to keeping
contact with our two girls, yet never altered,
strangely, my name. Of all things that for better

or worse she'd undertaken, that alone
she kept, perhaps feeling it proof
of having once been loved and so being worthy
of love again; or perhaps more her own
than that her father left, got by observing
not custom but free choice - a deeper truth.

So she lives still defined, given form, *created*
by the choice we once made. The name goes on
not as the tribal, clan-invoking badge
of birth, but like some ruined abbey fated
to stand unused, its roof destroyed by age
yet drawing dignity from what is gone,

though never to be restored. And for those others
on whom her life may chance, perhaps this long-
buried-in-past-time label, kept by choice
for what it means, bundled with nothing further,
may stir a presence which, through time's dank noise,
sounds in their lives some faint, love-echoing song.

Union Pacific

From space I watch the world
spin in her streamer dress,
wrapped like a dancing girl
in blue, green, golden tulle
so beautiful
that dizzied eyes forget
I am a part of her.

From a fringed Canadian train
snaking the Rockies I see
iced engine ahead and then
other coaches far behind me,
and sense – strangely, most in rain –
that I form part of them.

By the storm-choked telephone
my lostness sits on brood
begging your voice to call,
scared lest my mind's catarrhal
clog seals you, too, in stone,
I being part of you.

Goodbye, Daughter

I totter up to the light,
the sky pewter with streaks
of day strangling the old, sick past,
and shuffle shower-ward.
What day is it? Was it yesterday she left
for her home, my elf of joy?
Or Monday, the day before? I can't sort it out.
It's so long since she stepped away,
solitary in winter.
Lucidity limps back. I enter
the lit-up world. It was yesterday
– a brief eternity
that shines out like spun glass.
I gulp. Daybreak has passed.
And this is Thursday.

St Kilda

If I died here what obsequies would matter?
Only the jutting cliffs, the screaming gulls
and louring sky.
All the exigencies, panics and battles
beyond this vast Atlantic waste grow dull
as forlorn echoes round these high,

splintering crags. The fall of government,
tyrant or junta makes a distant sound
– a film in the next room,
muffled and pictureless, with no content,
no voice. This woman only, and this ground,
my world; my requiem, this billowing gloom.

Toys

To shelve for the last time the Barbie doll,
the fluffy white seal and stuffed Pomeranian
bigger than either daughter ever was
is to feel the pang of reading a mother's will
which marshals bequeathed wealth, when all that matters
is past bequeathing, gone on a last, missed train.

Moved by loss, I watch the two as they
stare in bewilderment at playthings stacked
in castoff-littered cupboard and oddment drawer
which once could spin the top of a summer's day;
and hear a small voice from one sister ask:
'Why don't we play with them any more?'

Which Way?

If causes *followed* effects
instead of going before,
then we could predict
a necessary cause,
without which there would be
no (earlier) consequence;
while causes merely sufficient
could be so various
we'd have no prescience
of the future's grip on us.
As things are now, though,
the opposite is true,
sufficient causes giving
(beforehand) power to view
ahead, the necessary not so
for others may be so, too.

Things could so easily go
backward – and be no worse –
if only God would throw
the world into reverse.

Disadvantaged

I wore a deerstalker and the kids at that
handicapped home called me
'the man with the funny hat.'
And what lodged in me like a thrown tomahawk
was that, while most of us
live anti-septic lives,
seeing misfortune as an acid bottle
spilled by some mischance on our chamois flesh,
suffering was these kids' norm.
And I realised how things stood.
Life hands its happiness out,
not equally – no, certainly not that –
but in a bell-shaped curve: most, in the middle,
get a good share; those at the ends much less.
It's an uncle at a party handing out goodies
but at time's end running low.
And one small girl came to me
– mop-headed, a slid-out eye, a sheepdog look -
and as if we'd long been lovers
held herself against me
in infant innocence, and begged that I should hold her.
Then she took my hand
in consolation, soothed, as if she knew
that in this pass-the-parcel game of chance
to be held in someone's love, of all we long for,
is the utmost life brings.

The Bad News

'To tell the truth, I never much liked it,' I heard him say,
his eyes still smiling, when the doctor's verdict came.
The ridge of his cheek furrowed and its crease
brought back, in a silent-movie flicker, the face
of the small boy he once had been. A flame
of joy that so little he cared for would cease

came to me with that sentence; and then sadness
that he'd gained no more to lose; finally,
disbelief, a sudden eye-gouged seeing
how little I'd known him across fifty years,
and how sick from early days his life had been,
though he still smiling.

Love

When my nose grew a bulb
after so many cocktails, so much partying
with Ronald's partners and guests,
he took the strawberry out.
When my tum was an inner tube
crumpled and pillowing,
his lancet renewed my youth.
When my breasts went asag
from seven kids
and failed the pencil test,
he sewed in these new cones.
When he's out at night
working all hours for me
I sit at the mirror and bite
back tears for the love he gives me.
More than that, though, I know
that on working weeks away
he'll never stray, not for long. Why
should he? If he tires of me
his knife, his suction and thread
can always make me new.
It's why I'm so safe with Ronald, so secure.
Really I am. You do see, don't you? *Don't you*?

Edgware Road, 7 July 2005

To have found the book meant so much to me.
For it showed you'd been reading in the train
and so wouldn't have looked up and seen his eyes
or the rucksack packed with whatever jelly
or powder he used to make my life in vain.
Death's blast felled you before you realised.

So you left, peaceful. There was no goodbye,
no glimpse of these long years in a silent house.
Lost in your book, its pages not yet charred,
from one dream-world your young imaginings glided
into another. The only difference now
is scarred in me. Ex-mother of you, ex-child,

I have become ex-priest. It wasn't that
I lost my faith in God – I still believe –
but in a forest clearing, privately,
not like a trumpet blown. And, wondering why,
I remember that the man who heaved
the killing rucksack, or who hung from a strap

on that Tube-sweaty morning believed he,
as I myself did, carried out God's will,
that he'd gain praise should he obliterate
those of another dream. My ministry
died from unease with faith, so versatile
equally to be turned to love or hate.

Dagmar

(A British spy enrolled in the Nazi Party, Eddie Chapman
after the war never returned to his Norwegian fellow-spy
and lover).

She never married, never had children;
and perhaps regretted not having his,
her British spy in Nazi uniform.
During those years of the occupation
stiff with the fear of arms-trade for the Resistance,
the war came first. She heard the whispers rustle
(but so that she heard), *'that German tart,'*
yet, sworn to silence forever,
she never slammed the lie, not even long after peace
alighted and the decades ticked away.
In her last years a niece was her sole support,
who never knew the past, till at Dagmar's death
she found in a ribboned box a flock of letters
written to him in English but never sent.
Hope took its time a-dying.
Deepest imprint of all, one day the girl,
entering a room in silence, found her aunt
dancing alone before a mirror.
And the still, slow movements, as if commemorating
hope like an infant's death,
were an ember of something loved that might have been
and held the girl in tears
as the interwoven waltz
grappled past pity's reach.

Doughboys, 8 May 1945,

We had rammed our tanks through the gates
and blenched to see them: men in striped prison-garb,
staring, too starved to cry; straw bodies tossed to mud
or stacked in putrid sheaves; three dangling a gibbet;
the entrail-wrenching nosegay; the experiments.
We had learnt the hard way to hate Germans.

Yet these, the cheering crowd, were German.
They wept, vibrated hand-flags – British, American.
A young, buxom woman climbed on the half-track,
lassoed me with a wreath of flowers and smacked
her lips like red figs into mine. And the melt of body
against body, the gratitude of arms and girl

crunched and half-cleansed the phantasms all around.
A child was lifted aboard and stuffed with candy
and an old woman faltered in English – her dead son…
she'd been so proud…and now…
In the city square a fountain and its basin
played grotto to naked youths and girls

in Pan-like ritual, all afire with it.
Hatred and love clashed. For they, too,
were liberated, just as we were. In them there'd been
two chemical sealants, uncongealable:
hope of a better world under the swastika
and fear of the door-knock in the night.

And for those unmixed water-oils, ours and theirs,
only one solvent rose, soaring in tears.

Granddaughters

That they live so far away
defeats my hopes. For I would like
those two small ladies through their lives
to pause one winter evening and mark
some little way of mine, some gleam of the eye,
or smile or cast of the face - the shade
coming upon it when they took their leave.

But time and distance, most of all
the effervescent, irrepressible spring
of youth and love and families
will ditch all that. And that, as well,
I approve. Why should so poor a thing
as thoughts of Paudeen crowd out loves like these?

Ammonite Fossil

Injected with strata of jet yet crumbling,
the cliff disinters entrails wet with spray
from the tongues of breakers lapping and yelping.
Small rubbles release their falls.
The truculent Whitby cost
snubs a cold-as-schooldays morning.

But you reawaken time. You grow shiny at rub of my
                                        thumb,
gemstone exhibit folded a million years
in your mattress bed.
Once, you clenched your shell tight and sank into night,
brain-dead within a sediment
of dream-exiling sleep.
Now, though, I feel you stir, shift with the tide,
rattling the shoulders of your fellow-stones,
their silt and clay-bands.
You never thought to awake
but now freeze, fearful of this weird ape's jolting,
the wounds of paw and trowel
and the cry of steel pterodactyl overhead.

Throwback

He throws bread from the tower each Saturday.
'Geezy,' the kids call out, 'you're potty. You're cracked.'
They cluster to watch and jeer.
'It's an old rite,' he pleads. 'Goes back
to Middle Ages times. Alms for the poor.'
'Now's not like that,' they say.

'Except for stuffing starlings, what's it do –
you chucking crumbs on t'grass
from mucky battlements?'
The question scalds – that they're so crass
more than its content. 'It's to care
for folk worse off than you.

It keeps the goodwill going.' Yet then there creeps
a wound into his hurt-by-blindness face,
a longing to tread again
ancient remembered woods, a place
whose hush, scratched only by cry of sheep,
pleads that we stop the train.

Not Out

It stood all his life on the mantelpiece,
its red seam and leather pores
perched on a stand of wood, a throne
declaring what he'd once been but now was
no longer, the matches won, runs scored,
the catches held. Every week
Mother dusted it, unseeing, and in the evenings he sat
beside its polished globe, dumplinged to fat
once inconceivable in the deep field
or coming up to bowl. At his decease
we faltered. What should we do
with this, his trophy? It had been
precious to him, and somehow
its value went on after he had left
- or he himself did – or its being on show
made him continue living. He'd be bereft
if it was ditched, or we would if we made
an end of what he'd loved, a knife-
cut to his flesh, his pride, the doubtful boast
of what he'd been in life.
And so it stayed, survivor
in its own place of honour, a messenger
tongue-tied for words, a never-opened letter,
a ball unfielded waiting its last throw.

Snow

I would have the world always like this.
All angles smoothed to curves
and, at the crests where shadows begin,
the coarseness of ground-glass crystals
abraded like the ill-shaven skin
of a gentleman of the road,
a rough of hedge and doss-house.

I would carpet the snowball globe
with this white whirlwind,
an eiderdown split wide open: above it, a blue sheet;
below, green grass lying hidden;
the pathways narrowed; the tops of walls
crowned with precarious toupees;
house-eaves baring their fangs
in serrated topples of ice;
the bowling green spotless, adazzle;
car-windows slowly lowering
their cottonwool sarongs asag at the middle;
the door-lock's gritty refusal.
And the silence. That above all
cleanses and wipes out the smudge
of traffic's growl,
If I were to conjecture paradise
I would not call up piddling fountains under Moroccan sun
nor the courts and labyrinths of the Alhambra
but would breathe the sweet smell of snow
and raise my eyes to Andalusian icecaps
spiking the way to heaven.

Brief Encounter

You're so clever, my daughter,
smuggling this little piglet from your tum.
It's more than any conjuror could do. *I* couldn't.
So I'm a grandad now. He turns
his grey pool eyes on me, weighs me up,
doesn't think much of me, perhaps,
but at length decides I'll do. I'm not important enough
to make complaint about or take back to the shop.
I wouldn't make grade as a dad but any old stick
will do for a gramp. He burps.
Quite. I don't blame you. He can't see
any future for a fellow like me.
And indeed there isn't much.
Yet maybe when my train draws out of the station
he'll turn on me those same pool eyes
and think of the fun times we had together
and wonder if he should have found out more
about the old codger who, dwindling now
at the carriage window, looks back at him
on the bare platform, seeing only a man
who left behind nothing of any note or value,
except memories. Which might redeem it all.

'Someone to see you.'

The students at my lecture sent me
a kissogram girl!
I'd hardly ended
when there, in front of the benches,
she stood like something a godmother-fairy
felt she could spare me –
new to my world!

Scantily clad. Her shoulders bare
and a bare waist
bordered a pair –
but modesty desists.
Arterial lips were what most caught my eyes,
those and full, rounded thighs
where all eyes gazed.

Before my jaw recovered, she'd
run up and kissed.
On my cheek's side
three inches wide
a rich, ripe, blood-red crescent marked me down
as rake-about-town
- a hedonist!

More scholarly researches showed
they'd had to pick –
could have employed
a roly-polygram devoid
of the svelte curves *my* girl displayed.
A strippogram would have made
a palpable hit!

But kissogram it was, and I
felt it was right
they should supply
a kiss to comfort my

Augean labours at the chalky board,
not dreaming they'd afford
me such delight.

Make-Believe

It isn't only kids. Grown-ups as well
adapt their roles, become what suits a place.
On Chester's walls
I'm a Catullus, conscript in the legion
Valeria Victrix, north wind in my face,
scouring Welsh hills,
eyes straining far beyond the river's swell,
heartsick for posting to a sunnier region.

London brings out the Boswell, the *rapport*
of coffee houses' warmth , the Kit Kat club,
all the world's thought
and half its famous men – Steele, Addison,
Johnson, Pope, Reynolds. All life's round its hub,
its cobbled streets. Far off,
NYC's guardian holds her lamp aloft
to tyrannised Europe's poor and downtrodden.

Nowheresville's doughnut shack is a wild west bar
where Blackfeet prowl and stalk. Nairobi's where
Lord Delamere
(Somali porters following) camps among
marshland and rippling streams. Berlin's a square
where Frederick's troops drill. Everywhere
history transforms, a boyhood den where fact
is lit by fancy, turning the present back
to brand-new past, making an old world young.

Balloons

After the obsequies, the fun.
Freed after requiem mass, we take off
black jackets, slot prayer books into pews,
invade the nearby park. Sixty balloons
- milk-white with messages trailing them like kites -
are handed out, released to soar in stately,
ever-climbing farewell, growing
smaller and smaller into endless sky – our
thoughts of Valerie. And these
will be picked up by children far out west
in Taunton, Cork, Cape Cod or Labrador –
cumulus ribbons on the silk road Val
believed she'd travel. The last bubble-dots
merge into cloud. We troop indoors for food.
And now the surge of unloosing. Old friends meet,
unbutton, learn what's happened, what became
of pals they've shared - 'Snorter' Smith, 'Bugs' or Trish.
Singles forage for partners. All the hunts,
chases and scents of throbbing life
come back redoubled, as if comradeship
switched on with one soul's loss. Does death
ratchet a squadron or battalion's grasp
on unity? Why do we pulse like this? Because,
all scores being cancelled towards the dead, the same
commonplace daylight's wary, starched distrust
towards the living dies, a prison door
pierced at first target practice?
Or is it that we feel righteous
at giving Val a send-off - we hug the sense
she's left us on a journey we find awe-filled
yet somehow safe because so universal? Hardly.
Deliverance comes mainly
as our reprieve, not hers, that we have fooled
death this time round, knowing full-time defeat's
already certain but, for now, fighting still.

Pied Piper of Hamley's

A rainbow army of puppets
but drilled in violence!
Action Man with his barrel trunk and biceps
fit to uproot sequoias.
The Terminator putting not *paid* but *cancelled*
to all opposing debt.
Guys of the Golden West, white hats, white horses
and white at heart. Yet always force
is their first quick draw, what they are reflex at.

Love? Not exactly. More, gloss sex lavished
on infant girls to varnish
their snowdrop days with nightshade purchases,
the *belladonna atropa* of nurseries.

And the pets – aren't they cuddly fun?
Stegosaur, maybe, with his triple tusk.
The Beast from a Thousand Fathoms crawling ashore
in the shudder of dusk,
hungry for tasty boys. Ape-men hordes,
and the Empire's elephants, their sahibs howdah-borne,
conquering with topi, Bible and Maxim gun.

Then later onslaughts,
enthroned or shadowed by the chattering squadrons
of Chopper, Chinook, spaceship or lurching Sherman.

I could gather this patchwork circus together,
a *White-Christmas*-crooned-on caravanserai,
and lead it to some mountainside
to tunnel there.
What would be left? Only the infancy
I once knew – with my three Christmas toys. One, a
wooden boat
my father planed, the sail stitched by my mum.
Second, *Radio Fun*.

And third beside them, loved as soon as known,
a parcel spied in some high, unreachable spot,
then past imagining – and now forgot.

Glasgow Necropolis: Best of Both Worlds

In tombs like houses, class pride glowers down
on tenements with that mixed attitude
of bullying and assurance that the trade
in fetid human flesh to the Caribbean
and sugar or tobacco back to the Clyde
righteously sanctified, hardened – and paid.

Yet why these vaults? Surely, with endless bliss
sealed by the Kirk, such black, pharaonic tombs
don't need to mark this vale of others' sins?
Unless that self-same urge, excess
of sureness of salvation, roared them in,
staking remembrance of crowns still to come.

Take-aways

They 'took me out of myself', those films of childhood,
engulfing me like Jonah in the darkness
of deep-pile palaces where usherettes
flitted, Greek goddesses bearing lamps,
and couples, here alone alone together,
launched fumblings of unbreathable intimacy
among the swashing buckles of pirate romance
or the pulse-jarring beauty of Margaret Lockwood.

And sometimes books would enthral
so that I drowned, mindless of time and company.
Bombed terraces could have blazed there, rows on rows,
or a spider lankied its way across my eyeball
but Lorna Doone would have reigned still, undeposed.

Games, too. The goldrush frenzy of Monopoly,
the petrifying magnetism of chess,
the happiness winning Happy Families meant.
Nothing now fires like the loyalty oath to Burnley
or Tom Finney at Preston North End.
Nothing bears me away like those waves
lifting and curling their locks round head and body,
washing castles to tooth-stump graves
on Filey beach or Skegness.

Joys for a season caught.
Now, in bus station or railway,
locked in the bleak, stale grey
of untransporting transport,
I long to be, once more, carried away.

Design Fault

The crane-like stiffness and ache
when I straighten myself to stand bespeaks
the spine's shaky scaffold for life.
No eyes at the back of my neck,
though surely that would be better.
And the belly with its addition
of a rupture-prone appendix,
a gadget fixed to the bus
for no known purpose or end,
a biblio-annotation
put in for show, not use.

So much of our body's like that.
The meanness that awards
a man only two hands. The chill
of furlessness, at least
in most mentionable parts.
And the excavable tonsils
in every standard model –
hidden interior bull-bars.

Most, though, the defile
through which we broach this world,
the newcomer's sole map.
How are we meant to climb
with lolled, disproportionate head
through a circlet of gristle-chained bones,
when any competent draftsman
would scurry back to his board
and correct so mad a plan
with a crackling Velcro flap?

To My Daughter

Gotten with so much pain,
so long a labour,
your mother values you
more for the grief you gave her,

repaying hurt with love.
Or perhaps it's we, unworthy
of one as bright as you,
who from that April birthing

to this December snow
without desert receive
from your cloud-rifting smile
love in exchange for grief?

Review

- How was it, then, for you,
the brief four-score?
- Like the turning of a page
or the way the morning tide
writes ripples in the sand
that vanish, smoothed away
before night falls.

Costs and Benefits

Excuse me, Miss, isn't your midriff cold
these January days,
rippling out in the frost
between your parting ways?

And those tight pants lining your thighs,
a second skin –
their seams slice tender spots.
Don't they dig in?

Forgive me asking, don't those conical bras
cramp you to space
all right for ice cream but for you
not the right place?

Those chest implants, M/s, surely seem
a suicide bid.
What risk at your age! Can young men
really be worth it?

Love, Hope, Recompense

Christmas Day. I recall how,
with the ward's bare, splintery floor
puddled with that bleak daybreak,
he lay suffused by the glow
of dripping blood, yet rather bore
waking than tried to wake.

To the end he thought he'd be
home for Christmas and yet
here it dawned – holly sprig,
the punctuative tree,
the nurses' mistletoe bet,
doctors in Santa rig –

and yet no leaving. Worse,
a gut-reaction to
his own past life retracts
all that he did and was.
Lifelong niggard, on two
young nurses he confers

cash gifts. And now to me,
not having moved a lip
these past five years, he stretches
a hand of fraternity.
Does he know it's all up?
Or is it hope that reaches

out past gaunt bones, an absurd
longing to brandish power
now to expunge the past
by gift or touch or word:
that every earlier hour
shall be changed by this last?

Dying, what an act means
was written long since, living.
Better to have the wit
to let doubt rest unseen,
so that there springs from it
only the good of giving.

Inventory for Andromeda

What shall we put in our spacecraft,
enfold what message in
its spidery gantry, to spin
beyond the last faint clutch
of the sun's fingers
in zero-gravity night?
We want nothing left
out of *Voyager*'s hold
that might make our message vivid,
our Earthling story bright.
There's so much, so much
we want to declare
to any creature out there
swimming ammonia seas
or borne up on sulphurous clouds,
its eyes perhaps nest-holes
for hydrogen-feeding birds,
or with muscles of living oil
that suck a gravelly twilight
from microbial canopies
in another universe.
I write it out in a verse:
We send our disc to you,
speaking an Earth-man's welcome
in a hundred languages, plus
others in which we're dumb
- that of the humpback whale
and its ocean-wandering crew
or the scatter and wheel and cry
of swifts as they set sail
on a journey as far to them
as Voyager*'s is to us.*
Here are images of ourselves,
our mountains, meadows, snows;
oceans, their trenches and shelves;
music and birdsong,

its pitch tuned by the electron
our world surely shares with yours.
But most, above all those,
our cargo brings tastes and scents
- flasks of wine, fresh-baked loaves,
perennial-flowering plants
each packed with the intent
to outwit time; and, most,
sugar-drink-drugged and heavy,
wallflowers' insobriety
and the blessing of a rose.

Desiderata

What I miss most about these autumn days
is the power that being changed,
or driving change, can bring
or the faith that it could be so: the stirring
of fox or wolf in the far-spread grassland prairies
that were one's youth; the future ranged

like Rockies dimly, bluely visible;
the breeze flaring one's nostrils;
the altar-vows of high commitment;
the first-time setting sail for the Orient.
But why not now? It's not impossible.
Limb, heart and bankbook all

call a sure countdown. It is me
who in some disused cellar of the mind
stacked with spent canisters *(Look before you... twice
shy...teach an old dog...)* stares blind eyes and won't try
spring's freezing sap-stream, stinging arteries,
the late resilience of the willow wand.

The Night DJ

Midnight to first grey light is my territory.
When darkness clacks the feet of the late-home wanderer
and what-the-hell cats exchange fur and suspicion
along the tops of walls, on roofs and in pungent alleyways,
I man the mike.
They're not empty, those icy nocturnal steppes
where regional voices bumble bonhomie
as full of loneliness as the lunchtime news
is full of deceit and death. Only the callers change.
Here are herds lowing in the gloom,
a Serengeti host: the insomnia-disconnected;
the blown-off-his-flywheel fruitcake; the mind-wrapped
                                        philosopher
unpicking thought as a prisoner unpicks hemp;
men whose true-blue necks redden with sunset; those
                                        whose teeth
life has kicked in. The old, the ill, the sodden.
Men whom love laid no claim to. Women no man has
                                        touched.
We never meet. But on my fortieth binge
letters like flocks of pigeons fluttered the postbox,
just as at times they weep, that same disembodied
catastrophe of voices, for the death of a soap-star
realer than any friend.
They're a grandstand crowd, a conglomerate scatter of
                                        atoms,
whose lostness we hear a mile off
as they *Never Walk Alone*.
They're my comrades every night until every daybreak,
joined in the galaxy of a far enigma,
the company of heaven.

And Yet So Far

A January night
with frost crisping the trees
and a full moon -
huge grandfather watch,
pendent, its chain unseen,
glaring a constable eye
over the still, cold reaches
of the nibbled edge of town.
And through the telescope
braced on my lawn I see
across that same moon-face
an aircraft prowl.
So near the moon it seems,
so far from earth.
It is probing, scanning
dry seas and rocky craters
on a golden lit-up desert.
Yet to them,
those men in the cockpit, abreast
of that silent, watchful eye,
the moon must seem far off
and only we
on this spinning orb, blue and green,
that whirls its shreds of white chiffon
about in a seven-veils dance
round my telescope and me
must seem so close.

Rain

She rang and asked to come round and I was glad
because of her simple genuineness and joy
and when she arrived rain glittered in her hair.
She asked, 'Did I still dance with Linda on Thursdays?'
And I said, 'No, we've changed to Tuesdays,' and knew
she'd asked some Thursday dancer and thought we'd split.

Then, how close were we? And I edged
out we were friends, no more. Oh, you could see
how the rain spangled her eyes! But when she said,
'Come back to me,' it was too sudden.
'I need to think.' 'You don't. The only thing
that matters is love.' But I wasn't to be hustled,

and now too late the rain
glistens its snail-track out of my own eyes.

Sugar Boat

(long since sunk in the Clyde
Estuary and now an island)

Barnacles, moss, worms,
gunge homes for foraging fish -
an eco-island moulded like brawn
is planted here
in this tide-racing estuary
round one sunk ship.
Salt-tinsel forms on the shark hull.
Trailed seaweed's borne,
like drowned girls' streaming hair, in queer
watery horizontality.

And here a new life-form's found like nowhere
else in the world, a slug-like sucker on
this sugar cargo.
As brine daily adds incompleteness,
grates on the sucrose shell, and pares
gnarled slivers from the hull's
once-stubborn iron,
new life is made, reminder of how
from wreck springs growth, from the strong sweetness.

Mary

In the orphanage she ate meals
of bread and margarine, drank gruel,
was herded in croc to school –
'the Muni' – a municipal disciple;
and at fourteen went into service. From that ordeal
at twenty-eight she married. And, as women did
in those bleak days, became a drudge
in her man's servitude, bore
the tyranny of his rages
in a house bitter with smoke.
Bore, too, three kids. Before they woke
in the dark of winter she had the fire lit,
grate polished. The whole house she fed
and clothed on four pounds ten a week.
Her life.
Now, at the Women's Fellowship
– chapel always her refuge – they hear it read.
'And I thank God' – her words –
'for all the many blessings he's conferred.'
Thanks – for that bleakness! The words
ring weird as Ouija
or talking to the dead
or thinking you'll be transferred
at death into some other creature
whose rank reflects your sins.
And yet it moves me that her thanks are sent
simply for being in this world: its scents,
its tastes and sounds, textures and tints,
the whole kaleidoscope of nature,
its brief duration, its escapeless end.

Reversal

The world assumes that when you scan
its faults with a disgusted face
you clearly think you're better than
those your frown marks out for disgrace.

In fact the opposite is truer.
The hanging precedents you favour
accuse yourself first, then transfer
their fire to damn others' behaviour.

It would be good, could it occur,
if, by condemning others less,
you might forgive yourself the more
and set the sentence in reverse.

For the Little-Read

Oh dear, what can the matter be?
Good bards are perishing latterly.
Sales gone to buy Lady Chatterley
strip all their royalties bare.

Now every publisher ceases
to read unsolicited pieces.
They all print unreadable theses
on Beowulf, Spenser or *Lear*.

Thousands of Ph.D doctorates
pour forth as kids (who know what they're at)
choose well-worn subject-protectorates
shunning the unknown and rare.

They choose for memorabilia
Shadwell's defunct juvenilia
rather than anything mealier
risking their college careers.

Passions the writer expresses
won't make a pile for the presses
but leave them with financial messes
American owners can't bear.

So damn all bards, say the critics.
They're hopeless at marketing gimmicks.
To starve hurts? Why then, they should quit it
And bask in a publisher's chair.

Retirement, Release

'Just calling in to get a mislaid book,'
he says. We nod, eyes lowered. No one believes
that from his home ten miles off Jock
drops in to get a book. He's here to relieve
the torment of retirement. Age
maroons him like an encircling, enemy tide,
barring the workplace that alone assuaged
his void of interests, wife, family, kids.
'Freedom is marvellous,' he says again.
We smile, a faint sweat spreading like a fan,
resist the pull of eye to wristwatch, and
we talk – or *he* talks – helping him pass the day,
his words panicked to speed at any sign
that we may grow impatient or move on.
'I've time for research at last.' He rubs
his hands, dry as his mouth, with fake
relish, much of whose working trouble
was the research blank. 'This is my great chance.'
We search in vain for signs of the mislaid book
in empty drawers while his bunched forehead cries
Just a sec more. But we see only hands
clawing the air for any human touch.
empty of hope as those wild, staring eyes.

Upper Room

'One of you will betray me,' he said,
and they halted, the bread halfway to their mouths.
In all twelve the words aroused
the same frenetic question: *Is it I?*
as if somehow the act of treachery
lay beyond will or motive.
Innocence dumbed them. The doubt was real
even in their twelfth mind. No one planned betrayal.
'The man now eating from the dish with me
will be the traitor.' Yet no one took
action to stop him or prevent
what no one wanted. Perhaps they knew by then
it was too late to stop the slide, the clock
already wound tight, past restraint.
For knowing of some coming event
always implies that those who know
can't alter or halt it. It isn't that foreknowing creates
powerlessness but that the gift alights
on those who have no power.
So its elect are Russia's Holy Fool,
dupe to the world, conned, bullied, ridiculed,
helpless to alter any angry throw
time's mocking croupier casts on the roulette wheel,
but repaid for the affliction of their souls
with special grace making the gashes heal,
only the helpless being gifted so.

A Hanging

'Stand just there, Derek,' I said. 'You'll be all right.'
How could I say it – *All right* –
as we edged him to the scales,
for final weighing?
We gripped his wrists and fastened them behind.
We'd thought to breathe free then,
when he couldn't fight, six feet of him that otherwise
could have wrenched an ugly scene.
But, meek as a sheep, he stepped forward and the
                                        meekness
made the deceit worse. My legs and belly were quaking
at the glib lie – not the lie itself;
that made him stand quiet, his face parade
the empty smile of a nine-year-old – but only
the act behind.
I thought of the judge, a man like this one, but wholly
avid for blood, to catch and hang
these long, child's-mind-linked limbs and vacant grin.
The narrowly clever had ensnared the inane
in salivating fangs.
Long years with rope and trapdoor had lodged in
my deepest gut a hatred
of what I did, yet for a moment the fierce
loathing wavered and I wished, instead,
this rope, this trap could see the wigged head swing.

Thoroughness

If Mummy had married Trevor, what would I
be like? Or Susan? Maybe I'd have those fat
rolls on my neck or white blotches under the eyes
like he does. I don't think I'd like that.
Perhaps it's just as well Dad came along
and bagged her, though she swears that anyway
she'd never have married Trevor – far too sly
and, in the house, taking up too much room
and always keeping her waiting far too long.
But you can't tell with Mum. She's very good
at not having dreamed of what she hasn't done
until another chance comes round, and then she does it.
Even with her marrying Dad I might be different.
And so might Susan. Prettier, or blonde hair,
or more like Princess Di – more radiant
and, well, princessly. Two kids don't go far
to show you what the possibilities are.
You'd need lots, *hundreds* probably, to say
how many'd look like Mum, or Auntie Prue,
or have Dad's eyes or nose. WHY HAVEN'T THEY
DONE THE JOB PROPERLY, had a dozen or two
at least? It's so exactly like grown-ups
to leave things half-baked. You can never trust
them to be thorough. I'll be thorough, though,
when I get round to marrying. Susan, too.

Mid-Life Stasis

Now, half my problems have gone,
vamoosed, caught the bus into town
without a by-your-leave.
Thank heaven! It's as if some local pain
who lived just down the lane
had his jaw turned to stone;
and I am free, bereaved
of nothing I'd want to own.

Youth's need to be like others
vanished like milk the cat drank.
All pressure to dress up, dance
or go to parties – all gone.
Even what had to be worn
wasn't freely chosen. Now I sport baggy pants,
a ragged sweater affronting decent folk,
down-at-heel shoes, a shirt no tramp would thank
me for providing. And the reason's plain:
I aim to impress fewer people but those few
to impress more:
the postman with my aerograms from Spain;
the gaping neighbours on my trampoline.
They think I'm dotty. And yet all the while
I'm simply putting on a personal style
- my little joke. I think.
I'm almost sure.

Giving Back

Among the penguin gowns and mortarboards
higgledy as begonia beds,
beneath the galleries of parental pomp,
the bulge-suit dads and flower-frocked mums applauding,
the absurd ritual droned.
We bowed. A Bible stained with the hair oil
of countless other heads baptised our crowns.
Dominus sic... The magic words once muttered,
we shuffled on. *Thank God that's over at last.*
And only decades later, half a lifetime,
I realised you weren't present, who paid for me
to attend that long-outdated seminary,
and how much you'd have given to be there
if only I'd thought
and overcome the shame of exhuming
you to my friends. Only now comes pain.
Youth can't unclamp its eyes to parents' pride,
only feels its own sweat. So the applause
wobbled reverberant round the vaults and ribs
of that aged pile, moving brimmed hats to quiver,
without you watching. And now you'll never watch
or hear my sorrow for the ingratitude,
the failure to feign pride, the stark rejection
of all you'd given.
Just as I, all those years past, never grasped
the hurt my blindness meted out to you.

Nos Et Mutamur in Illis
(for Rose, who revisited Auschwitz)

We stood here. On this ground,
this ordinary clay,
our hands scraped out the sound

that sent others each day
to bleak winds, purple lips
and bone-racked drudgery.

Privilege. That was it.
To play in the camp band
while others hewed with pick

or hacked with bleeding hand
at rock-face or pine-tree
brought to this death-palled land

a filtered humanity.
What difference can we know
between now and that day?

The spot's the same, as though
some commandant or guard
could appear and with low

broken accents command
prompt death or slow decline
to the same shuddering end.

What's changed is only mind.
Nerve and brain cells have grown
more gentle, more refined.

We hear the wind's sad moan
like our once-saving sound,
yet it's still hard to own
we stood here, on this ground.

Turtle Station.

Night, like a sweatshirt. Total silence
but for the China Sea's offhand
throwaway swill. Nerve-tensed, we wait
the coming invasion with a sense
of ocean monsters striking land,
and yet with awe, a wanting not to hurt

these age-old denizens of the deep.
Something moves at the beach's edge,
snagging our breath. And then they come.
Laboured and lumbering, they creep
upshore and, limestone armour lodged
on sand, fall prostrate. They've come home.

Flippers scrape, ill-directed. Slowly
a basin hollows out. We bend
by brittle stars' tinsel and peer
at the senescent mother. How lonely
she must be at this marathon's end,
her thousand miles alone. Yet here,

unaware yet encircled, from her fall
drops like a desert spring, a flow
of warm, soft, shell-less eggs, the sum
of her year's toil. The theft of all
her harvest she seems not to know
but, a backed truck, flails around to resume

the life-tide of her to and fro.
From this brief night-call summer will see
sixty – a hundred – leathery sprogs,
new-hatched, scuttle and skitter across
night's beach to where, knee-deep, we hold
torches and, so lit, start the way

their never-met-with mother took.
What courage – to embark alone
on such a swim, its predators
and pitchy, swallowing depths! What luck
if, from the purge, a few live on,
prompting reflection that the cause

of valour like that must be always
to swim one stroke at a time, to broach
one hour. And with it a sad sense
that such assailant courage may
owe much, too, to a dim approach,
buying its dauntlessness with ignorance.

Tenement

Rumble of rats in the wall. Five storeys up,
she swallows. Hair askew
as a worn toothbrush, eyebrows nipped with fear,
she bounces – a volt for each of her seventy years –
to thump the lurking menace under the plaster,
then sits, ashudder at her sole companions.

Company comes when evening carpet-unrolls
haar from the Pentlands' tumuli.
Then, among steel-tubed chairs in a medium's shadow,
she aprils tears
of love to him for whom she turned down love,
father, with tar-black hair and muscled throat,
her long night's only star.

Alpine Man,

imagine yourself new-born,
Levered with picks from ice
warmed by the masseur sun
back to a new, old life.
Three thousand years haven't changed you.
Your limbs are sinewy still;
But your eyes, narrowed for prey
- mastodon, mammoth, fox –
transfix a different world,
milder, shorn of ice-lock,
glacier, avalanche, cave.
And the warm wind! Green trees! Flowers!
Your first, stiff steps rejoice
in the solid earth; you breathe
the gratitude of the air.
And all you meet
in street, town or market stall
so straightforward, so guileless-seeming.
It's the first, hushed day of spring,
it's your eighteenth birthday,
it's the tide coming in
before the town's astir.
And all you have lost
is memory. You know nothing
of the ages when you lay
in your ice sarcophagus
awaiting this latter day.
You bear no scars
from snub, spat, scorn, surprise.
No one has savaged you,
no one deceived, despised.
Alpine man, weep your good fortune.
Enjoy these infant days
with no past load, no burden
borne from the chaingang past,
but sprite-free, unaware

of the debts that will outlast
your rebirth, that will bow
your back before you know,
blind to what threatened once
and all that darkens now.

Eternal Triangle

What does she say to God,
this woman I married?
I see her every night
(except, strangely, abroad)
kneeling, a little harried,
as if a show of haste
will somehow serve to hide
the earnest act's importance.

What does she ask? Is it waste
of words bringing no response?
Or has He ever replied?
Does my life gain some light
from prayers to keep us safe
- *Defend us from all perils*
and dangers of this night –?
Or does she pray to save
me from becoming evil,
her words twice-blessed, repelling
inward, as outward, danger?

Whispers sound: *...kingdom come...*
thou who knowest the hearts of
all men... I listen, a stranger
shut from this intimate room,
a duo I'm no part of,
lodger in my own home.

And yet I never ask.
Questions would strike a blow
down on this strange, eternal
lopsided triangle.
Better that I don't know
than that I live to feel
a second, separate void

at lacking power to heal
double-love, once destroyed.

Identity

They followed me along,
six of them, not barefaced
or cheeky-challenging
but wide-eyed as if amazed.

Then halted in a line
at someone's garden gate.
I too stopped, to divine
how awe could be so great

for a lone leafleter.
Till a boy stepped forward and said
(aged seven, perhaps – their leader),
'Are you Eleanor's Dad?'

And then at last I realised
why the dumb-stricken awe.
The identity I prized
- professional, learned in law,

the much-admired CV –
was so much empty blather.
My real identity
was being Ellie's father.

And a strange pang of pleasure
came and remained that night
- still does at times of leisure –
a setting of values right,

a knowing, however often
home-role or work's at fault,
one thing will always soften
and bring regret to a halt:

the certainty that whether
life turns out good or bad
nothing I do will ever
compare with being a dad.

Lies

'I came last month,' she tells me.
Yet only now she phones.
Why the delay? She fears that,
single now, I'll propose.

She wants no re-fired passions
spoiling her UK stay,
so rings her old companion
just as she goes away.

Propose? A strange illusion
that makes her edgy and shy,
keeping her distance. Wounded,
I choose to tell a lie.

I say,'I've found a partner.'
At once the fencing ends.
Lies, see your value to me?
You give me back my friends.

Words That Say Nothing

'How do you do?' I say, and you reply
'How do you do?' Or I say, 'Well, well, well.'
Sometimes the best response is, 'My oh my,'
to some indifferent story people tell.

Words that say nothing. Should they be suppressed,
struck from vocabulary as redundant?
'Really?' 'No kidding?' 'Well, who would have guessed?'
No, it's not trickery makes them so abundant,

or wanting falsehood hidden in what's said.
Words like these carry warmth, keep business flowing.
They can't spark discord. Why not keep them, then?
Meaninglessness? One of the best things going.

Valentine

I found a rose waiting outside my door,
blossoming, scarlet-new
at this mid-winter rift.
The single stem startled and moved me more
than most rich presents do,
giving my heart a lift.
I felt more worthy of love, a bit more grown,
the giver being unknown.

Not knowing's half the gift.

Truth

'He's busy, Tina. He has lots to do.'
What hurts is that look in her eyes. Her life
turns on her daddy's coming. Now she says,
'Where is he? Will he come for holidays?'
How can I answer?
I can't say, *Tina, he doesn't think of you*
any more now. He has another wife,
another little girl. But still the questions
gather and break. Memories from before the split
claw back her plangent voice like a refrain.
Why does my Daddy hit me?'
Oh, slam the door on truth! How can I tell it
when worship's in her face, longing to love
the violent drunk whose one act at conception
seems to her kindled eyes enough
for her to call him father? 'Tina, perhaps he'll come
and take you to the zoo one of these days.'
But self-hate gathers for the hope I've loosed,
the evasive phrase, the eel of treachery,
black bile passing its sentence equally
on guilt of hiding, or of speaking, truth.

Ten Days Before

Ten days before, they gathered. Six of them:
her mother, father, best friend, and the man
to be her husband. The priest read out the texts:
forsaking all other...till death do you part.

No guests, no choir. No others to forsake
for her who was to forsake life so soon.
No honeymoon, only the barred steel bed
hastily curtained off from a hushed ward.

I do. A blessing. The others retire
and they're alone together, newly-wed
with new vows, starting on the trek of marriage
that should have changed so much, now sliced so short.

And yet some spring stir seemed to fill
her papery cheeks, the rapid-taken breath,
some sense of purpose or fulfilment, dreaming
of wider seas than this lonely, wheeled vessel

could sail, some huge constructive act completed
that set a seal upon that hour of grace
when only the invisible was given
and when so little, yet so much, took place.

Blessed Siren

Singing alone in consort,
holding a line through catacombs of notes
tightens such rein upon the nerves
and mind, screwed down to tempo and timbre and pitch,
as not to notice others.

So, when the blitz ends and the all-clear sounds
I peer from out my concentration shelter
and scan the debris and shock
of other singers round,
stunned that I'm not alone.

Loyalty

He's not their kid at all,
just found and unreclaimed.
Small for seven years, his neck roped with long scars
where blows have blood-caked, he still calls them
Mum and Dad.
Knows to hide when they foot him out
from the cramped room. There's escape down there,
their gruntings barely heard, a distant grumble.
And the insect buzz
of the gross cylinder is a tropical night
sweltering his flank in the chill cellar.
'You'd like to leave?' the social worker asks.
He shakes his head, narrows hurt, anguished eyes.
'I want my Mum and Dad,' he says again.

Rainfall

Not merely not so unkind as man,
this downpour sluices, swills, absolves away
all man-made pain.
As the street scurries for shelter to doorway,
shops' tear-streaming glass plate
and rustle-protesting, impregnated trees,
it brings a rug of comfort to flee,
capsuled within one's own escape,
from worry, embarrassment and scam,
safe under raincoat, brolly or cape,
uncrossed, uncontradicted, unseen,
a wholly uncontested man.

Glad refugee not from this flood
but what the flood relieves,
I huddle and watch
its sheets shimmy down in disregard
of streetlamps' blotch,
exhilarant, its sodden leaves
dancing in their rags a galliard
of pure redemptory mood.

At home within the hour we
will shed clothes' slime and stand
steaming in front of fires, peeling away
social distress and wound,
conflict, anxiety, strain
– city-states faced with one dark enemy,
who in dire rout are joined
by this dividing rain.

John Donne
(a portrait purchased for the National Gallery, 2006)

Lean, opportunist face
with your razor moustache
and gleaming assessor's eyes,
we have you now,
held as that rangy, undressing stare
holds us, cool and too knowing,
experienced beyond all paths
our lives could take, your poems passed
from hand to hand, your hands from breast to breast.
Born to a world where faith
suckled on blood, an imprisoned brother slain,
an uncle quartered, wielding your sword
against Cadiz, then marrying
secretly in a flight from scandal's pry;
finally, with changed vows, your words
branding our minds – *no man an island...*
for whom the bell tolls...an equal music -
read from baroque and convoluted pulpit
with that same sad half-grin.
You never knew what age you lived in,
unveiler of all things else – the God-shadowed nave
of Middle Ages or the quicksilver dart of light
in the Rebirth; never knew
what faith, what love to grasp for;
nor any incised solution
to this vast cloud-complexity
of time, love, death, remorse,
in a life so tactic-sure, so object-lost.

Dear Descendant,

If you've nothing better to do, look me up.
In your far-future age there'll be a website,
an archive pine-needled with people's lives
from the forest-floor of the past, a landslide of days.
Search, access, riffle. Glaze your eyes with scanning.
Scour the registers of time, forgotten dates
creased in the flimsy pages of the years
where births and deaths alight. Turn the windmill sheets
of newspaper and mag for small achievements,
census returns, forms for homes and families.
(Note the piping infants who, like midday crickets,
fall mute between one sounding and the next).
Follow the work-trail – firms' and ministries' records
in dusty cellars, warehouses and lofts.
See how the genes wriggled their way
through a filigree of women,
often spilled from the watercourse of marriage,
till it reached you. Feel the ebb of generation,
epoch, strike, war, a magical transformation
clogged in the centuries' cobweb-curtain of rime.
Then, before dried lungs choke in gathering twilight,
look me up (dead leaf, otherwise forgotten)
if you've no better way to fill your time.

Pompeii

The couple lie entwined
just as they did when the torrent
of ash engulfed, consigned
to bi-millenial sleep.
Now, touched by the first wind
to graze them since all horror
choked their hot breathing, side
by blackened side they keep

their momentary vows
of love's eternity,
which perhaps neither one
dreamed would outlast the night.
He, portly and rich, may have owned
thoughts she'd be best led on
by gifts of jewellery,
now clutched too late for flight.

She, a young slave-girl. See?
On her finger a ring
marking his ownership
or showing special favour.
Only they failed to flee
the hungry flood ensnarling
this lodging house's cheap
refuge. At the last they wavered,

alarm springing too late.
Sandals lie unattended
beside the bed. Their fate
stands open, unamended,
for every age to see.
Time's eyes will gloat and pry
over the passions they
veiled in all privacy.

Softly, I stoop to inspect
her hand's dry, separate bones.
I touch the ring. No words
can tell what pity attends
this long-too-late respect,
what cry to make amends
to these shy, quiet lovers,
spent-drowsing, deaf to the groan

of the coming tide. Her charms
leaving no fragrance, his mind
unknown in its intent,
caution us who survive
(so prone to each other's arms)
that our end, undesigned,
the wish that our acts live
may not come as we meant.

The Hint

This is open sea miles from the pointing finger
of South-East Asia, the divide
of Indian from Pacific water.
Yet calm. These posts where fishermen linger
and throw their nets out wide
from moored boats seem to offer

promise that the waves can't go beyond
ten feet in depth, a warm
developing tray where bright fish swarm
and spindly house-stilts stand
like toes that grasp the sand
where the grab of tide scrabbles against the shore.

The bottom's too deep to glimpse
and yet we have the feeling
great waves won't surge here.
The comforting warmness hints
at shelter and security
over a flooded plain where gulls are wheeling

and crying as if in uncertainty
that Asia's hugeness can dwindle down to this.
Heart hugs this almost-island, this oasis
in the vast China Sea,
the start of love a dog's wagged tail gives,
the glimpse of a girl's thigh above the knee.

Fort McMurray, 2016

The headlights burn. A molten ridge
like a sand-furrow at low tide, appears
in the windscreen's glass. We put on speed,
shoulder-charging the blaze. To our rear
a wounded pine, turned black from green,
shoots photons of flame to another, a bridge

of fire passed like a rugby ball
before their splinters crash. A town
surrenders to heat and drought. And through it all
- the thumped accelerator, the pungent tyres
burrowing in ash like a skidding plough –
the image that recurs is how

two winters back this place lay under snow,
the house-eaves icicled like a frozen face
and a man who leaned against a window
supernova'd with crystal forget-me-nots
snapped and then fell, log-stiff, in the billowing froth,
a matchstick where the tongues of fire now blaze.

Piecing England Together

Through parted curtains from deep under
a snowdrift of duvet at High Torrent Barn
in a nestling Pennine crevice
my eyes travel over
a world of white-padded moor. And I wonder:
That flat-topped peak, cake-iced by last night's storm..?
Then, half-incredulous, I realise
It's Ingleborough!

Through a daze, the map joins up. This sentinel
I've climbed before from the Yorkshire side
and now, like stumbling on
the Nile's source on some Ethiopian hill,
I rediscover - an old-time mate whose pad
I've passed a hundred times, unknown,
whom I meet now, living cut off and alone
yet unmistakeable and recognised.

And it is like another country, this
uplifted moorland where the cries
of birds are all one hears and you realise
that but for tarmac England is a bog
and that that's all you want. Enrugged
in this barn's (but for the kitchen) ice
under the heavy fall of duvet, I lie napping,
a carefree dormouse, simply being happy.

My Novel

People are puzzled when I look at them
in my analytic, Sherlock Holmesy way,
sizing them up,
cutting them down to size,
giving them the once-over
twice or three times.
They don't know they're characters in my novel,
personae dramatis
because I keep my masterpiece
utterly secret.

Ponsonby doesn't realise that his hatred
of Price in Invoicing appears in Chapter Five
in the form of a murder
too gory to relate
to readers of sensitive disposition,
too shocking with blood and guts
to describe in a family poem.
Which is why, despite the sales
the full details would clock up for my best-seller,
I keep it quiet.

Adams in Adverts, who's having it off with Paula
in the Art Department and often appears
with lipstick bloom on his collar
needn't have any worries
that his wife, racing through my page-turner
on her annual Virgin express to Budleigh Salterton
to see her mum
and get away from Adams,
may recognise herself and take him to court
for defamation.

Anyway, the torrid scenes, though steamy
and hugely arousing, are carefully shrouded
behind drawn curtains;

the hero himself
– a veritable Apollo of the bedsheets –
is barely to be recognised as Adams
(except by Adams himself, who believes he is
an X–certificate hero);
and my novel keeps the sex scenes and their murmur
(from modesty and because my memory's failing)
entirely a private matter.

And so the benefits of the *magnum opus*
with its glorious, bloodthirsty, hotbed scenes
accrue entirely to me,
not at all to Ponsonby or Adams
and still less to Paula
or Mrs A or Price in Invoicing,
for only I know in my deepest heart the dastardly,
white-knuckle, bodice-ripping, breathless plot
of the novel I'll write one day.

Minister

Twice a year he comes, in April and October,
my Billy's father. I clean the house,
scent it with flowers, make the windows shine
with reflective memory. When his taxi burbles
round the street corner like a bumbling neighbour
we scramble and storm the door and Billy climbs
on to the garden wall. Excitement bubbles us.
We fling arms wide,
flurry the pavement's breadth while Billy throws
himself into Karl's arms. He knows
his Dad better than I. I smile, but timorously,
only half-acquainted even now
with the man who, seven years ago,
knocked on my door. 'I'm from the agency…'
So, failed in the search for love
and in harrowing flight from childlessness,
with prim formality I undressed,
lay between sheets and called him to come in.
And so the deed was done.
Karl's forty, a big man. He is paid nothing.
His only interest, he says, is helping
people like me, the lonely or fallow,
the sole, the unentwined.
Fifty-eight children he has, charts fifty-eight lives
– mop-headed, boisterous, shy, scarecrow or trim,
infant or at school or work –
and dabs each one a visit once a year.
So close a stranger. When he went
– by taxi again, our centrifugal link –
it's like the doctor going, or the priest,
proper, restrained and easy, the blessing given.
I awaited Billy by the calendar
and was fulfilled. The only loss, I sense
now, is Karl's own,
waiting these decades in his ministry
not finding love.

On Becoming a Grandad

You lie in your young mum's womb,
a buried mine, an explosion-in-waiting,
soon to be loosed on the world.
Only five weeks now.
I feel an urgency and a helplessness
to tell you all you need know,
to warn you of what you may meet,
to iron out naivety,
trust in wrong people, the crooked smile,
the small print under the breath.
I want to guide, to prevent you wasting your powers,
help you choose right amid the arm-twisting
and the jabbed stiletto,
yet still to hold faith in men.
You'll be possessed by your own life
but you need what I've learnt, need to know me,
so that when blurred acetate startles memory
of the hour of your grandad's death
you won't feel, too late, a wish
that you'd asked what I'd done with my days,
then, the wish ditched, walk on,
a stranger along the street
who passes by and then wonders
if I was someone somewhere you once met.

Given, Taken Away

(for Wilko Johnson who, diagnosed with cancer, went through with his tour of Japan)

A light snow is falling
over the pink-and-white cherry blossom
and icing-capped pagodas
of a Kyoto spring;
and behind the cherries
and their gloss of ringed bark, mountains
gather flakes on their crowns
as a seaman is streaked with foam on the high rigging.
I stand and breathe the smell
of snow, hear the silence of light.
Normally – but what is normal now? –
I would have settled all this in memory,
a book to return to, a photo for the future;
but now time's guard has slipped
and I have lived only one ticking moment,
over and over,
swum again and again in its unrecallable shallows
and for the first time ever, I am happy.

Plus Ca Change

From the top deck of my bus outside Victoria
I saw him walking, slightly bent,
briefcase in hand, up towards Hobart House.
Good heavens, I thought, *it's the man whose story I
heard from his own lips in north Tashkent.*
An accountant, he was, a man of some enterprise

who'd worked in Abadan under the Shah
and done a stint in Java. How odd
to find him at the same old Gaza-mill as me,
being so far-flung. But then I saw:
firms need accounts drawn up all round the world
and just as men fall into line – or cemetery –

in any dictatorial hell, so numbers
need drilling everywhere, lined in their smart platoons,
neat and subservient for the auditors.
The fact my landlord is Baluchi doesn't mean
he charges less, or wants more rent or sooner,
than if he were Kashmiri or Viet-Minh.

Migration changes nothing. Soon, my friend
stopped his laborious walk and turned aside
into *The Farmer's Arms,* near where the Queen
stays when in town. And I saw again
that double lives, like Double Diamonds, unite
The Crown and Pike, The Duke and Serf. That seen,

I hopped off early to *The Farmer*'s joint
and downed a plutocratic (yet plebeian) pint,
keeping all the time a predatory eye
out for my Tashkent pal. Who'd disappeared,
perhaps to Mali or Samarkand, while I
was left to wonder where the Farmers were.

Cortege

One hearse. One car. One mourner.
And the rainswept street deserted
by chance or through the calendar or day
or deceived by a trick of the light.
In a way, does it matter?
Either the dead man's away
to some cloudbank of content
moving like a landslide
of strings in a great orchestra,
or a billow in some curtain of hail
that parts to let sunlight enter;
or else he walks in a yellow muffling freeze
of nothingness, an envelopment
quite separate from his life, a haze
that forgets alike past, present, future days.
Either way, he won't fret
at only one soul remembering. He might
have been 'a gentleman of the road', sleeping lifelong
in a cardboard box in some doorway
or other joint where tramps gather to doss
in Shoreditch or New Cross.
Or perhaps his life at first went like a bomb,
gurglingly happy in more ways
than a later-ditched marriage and the loss of sons
could ever quite erase. Who is to know?
But does it matter that almost no one
missed him at death? Certainly all he did
(all that *we*'ve done) gains not a glint of worth
from those we impressed (or tried to),
not those absent at death
nor those with him, now gone
in hearse and car. Only the life lives on.

Nocturne

You perch on my arm
and we go round the room
each evening at bedtime. I say,
'Goodnight, clock. Goodnight, table.
Goodnight, chair. Teddy, good night.'
And you, nearly one now, have learnt
to repeat my gentle goodnights
and as you do
you become earnest and grown-up
so that I stop thinking it's childlike
to talk to lifeless things
but instead feel grateful and glad
that you give me excuse
to show my thankfulness -
a blessing I don't have
with eighty years now gone
and without you, circling alone
round the darkening room,
the house, the world, my life
saying, 'Goodnight. Goodnight.'

Paradise

Pocked sand, and streamlets probing the neck;
the school cap set on pudding-bowl-cut hair
defenceless against the sideways slant of rain;
the beach a contortion of abandoned deckchairs.

All unnoticed by me,
field marshal crouched in the building of sand harbour,
pebbled castle, moat and curtain wall.
For this was summer and Scarborough

and the fortress must be strengthened to withstand
downpour and the growling lick of tide advancing
with rhythmic drench or drained-away retreat.
And tomorrow the sun would be dancing.

Kin

Today, after the rattle of earth
on the casket, after the slow
return of ashes to ash, we move to the hall,
swept by a strange relief. Now,
in my family's home-place for four centuries,
no one of our name survives. No births,
no creaking grannies, no cries
or whoops from children playing ball.
I meet intimate strangers, cousins, nephews, not one
living within the ten-mile circlet
that once was the outer limit
of village travel. No one here will die
in the same house they were born in. And I
feel a giddiness at the loss of something
I never knew, the deep assurance and comfort
of tribal blood. Tonight, I'll shut
the door of my dovecote flat – at a height
my parents never scaled – and lie
walled near scarcely-spoken-to neighbours,
who, when I die, will find me some weeks later
and wonder who I was and who might care,
only distressed by my long lying there.

Christmas Eve

At nine it was time for bed
to claim Fay and young sister Joy;
and, setting aside Colonel Mustard
and his dastardly deed in the Library
with the lead piping, I said,
'Better douse down the fire. It would be hard

on Santa to leave it burning.'
And so there, near the cooling ash,
we laid out food for our guest
who would come when we had passed
into magical, blessed
dreams of the old year turning
to future, better things. And with the girls in far-
away deep-sea slumber, I ate
Santa's cake-slice and plum, and left
a bite in the carrot where the reindeer
could be seen to have had his share, only distressed
that Fay, now seven, might guess
how far truth and magic part.

Darkness Visible

Through shimmying curtains of rain, under night-sky
molten with lowering cloud
the cop cars come.
Their headlights swing and plunge, seeking out some
cause of unwonted traffic on the Glendour Road.

Drug dealers? Sheep thieves? They splatter to a stop.
The men in cagoules shade their eyes
against the lights. Capes jack-knife back the glare.
As if barely noticed, the cops
cluster at the telescope. In vertiginous air

above thermos and breath-cloud, high
in a hole trenched in the sky's depression, the prize
the men have found is the Crab nebula. The cops are taken
aside
like visitors half-expected
and told that, shelving oft-detected

Russian or US satellites,
now, in a thwarted frenzy of hopelessness,
genocide's on to free the Borders' night
from all that stains the heavens, man's glow that wipes
a million stars from view, for lightlessness,
the abyssal dark which alone gives men sight.

Curriculum Vitae

How was it, then, for you?
Like something that took place
in the mist of dawn today
but now seems a year ago. Like some
mothball scent in a drawer
of lavender from last autumn,
now scattered far away,
a dream you can't locate
in the obits of the years.
Like a huge evening sky at end of summer
which a child reaches to grasp,
a past that is never
one with the clay-clogged present,
no canvas in the gallery
of real-life things
– that erosive trickle of grit,
those huge gambles for such small winnings.
In the rear-view mirror it dwindles,
a Tantaline fruit that's gone
at the touch of grasping lips.
Yet yesterday's taste hangs on,
giant in stature, but deceiving,
a barrage balloon aglitter
with silver foil of huge purpose,
hoist for tonight's raid and yet yielding
no promise of any dawn.